CAUSES, SYMPTOMS AND TYPES OF SCHIZOPHRENIA

Knowing the best drugs treatment for schizophrenia..

By

Dr DOUGLAS JASON

TABLE OF CONTENTS

ABOUT THE AUTHOR

Dr. Douglas Jason is a certified dietician who has a strong passion for wellness and a big eagerness to help people all over the world. He uses healthy food, herbs, spices, and other useful tools to help mankind realize its overall goal of optimum health.

INTRODUCTION

Schizophrenia: What Is It? Schizophrenia is a persistent, severe, and crippling mental illness marked by irrational ideas, strange behaviors, and antisocial conduct. Because schizophrenia is a psychotic condition, the individual who has it occasionally loses touch with reality.

CHAPTER 1

Who Is Affected.

A little more than 1.1% of people worldwide suffer from schizophrenia.
Schizophrenia affects 3.5 million people in America.
Most cases of schizophrenia are discovered between the ages of 16 and 25.
Schizophrenia may run in families (runs in families)
Men are affected 1.5 times more frequently than women.
Schizophrenia and its treatment have a significant negative

economic impact, costing anywhere
from $32.5 to $65 billion annually.

CHAPTER 2

Schizophrenia Types.

(Infant)
Rarely do young children develop schizophrenia. Only one in 40,000 kids, according to the National Institute of Mental Health (NIMH), develops schizophrenia symptoms before the age of 13.

Schizophrenia has five different subtypes (discussed in the following slides). They are divided into groups based on the symptoms that the subject displays during the assessment:

schizophrenia with paranoia
chaotic schizophrenia
schizophrenia with catatonia
schizophrenia that lacks distinction
Chronic schizophrenia

schizophrenia with paranoia

Paranoid behavior, such as
delusions and auditory
hallucinations, distinguishes
schizophrenia from the paranoid
kind. Feelings of persecution,
surveillance, or association with a
famous or notable individual, such
as a politician or celebrity, or with an
organization like a company, are all

signs of paranoid behavior. Anger, anxiety, and hostility are common behaviors in people with paranoid-type schizophrenia. The individual typically exhibits fairly typical affective and intellectual expression.

CHAPTER 3

Schizophrenia Causes.

There are numerous, interrelated causes of schizophrenia, which might vary from person to person.

Genetics (runs in families) (runs in families)
Environment
Cognitive chemistry
previous abuse or neglect
Solutions For Health From Our Sponsors

increased risk of stroke
Discover a New ED Treatment for Severe UC Using Immunotherapy.

Think About This Surgery

There is a hereditary component to schizophrenia. While just 1% of the general population develops schizophrenia, 10% of persons who have a first-degree family (parent, sibling) who has the condition do. If an identical twin also has schizophrenia, the chance is higher. Additionally, those having a second-degree family (aunts, uncles, cousins, grandparents) who have the disease are more likely to experience it.

CHAPTER 4

Schizophrenia Symptoms.

Many schizophrenia sufferers don't seem to be ill. As the illness worsens, the person will exhibit a variety of behavioral changes that will make them appear 'off'. These signs include:

Social isolation
Anxiety\sDelusions
Hallucinations
Feelings of suspicion or persecutory intent
lack of appetite or skipping meals
decline in hygiene

The categories that can be used to classify symptoms are covered in the following slides.

Positive Symptoms (More Overtly Psychotic)
The "positive" symptoms, which are those that are psychotic and are not present in healthy people, include:

Delusions
Hallucinations
Unorganized speech or conduct
defective mentality
other movement abnormalities, such as catatonia

Negative Symptoms of a Deficit

"Negative" symptoms interfere with regular feelings and actions and include:

Social isolation
Lack of facial expression, monotone speech, and "flat affect"
inability to convey emotions
inadequate self-care
unavailability of pleasure (anhedonia)

Cognitive Signs
The most challenging symptoms to identify are those involving the brain, such as:

inability to make decisions and process information

inability to concentrate or pay
attention
memory issues or difficulty learning
new activities

Mood or affective symptoms
Mood-altering symptoms are
referred to as affective symptoms.
Schizophrenia patients frequently
have concurrent depression and
may act or think suicidally.

CHAPTER 5

How Is Schizophrenia Diagnosed?

The diagnosis of schizophrenia is determined both by excluding other medical conditions that could be the source of the behavioral symptoms (exclusion) and by observing the presence of the disorder's distinctive symptoms. The doctor will check for the presence of social withdrawal, dysfunction at work or in everyday activities for at least six months, as well as delusions, hallucinations, disorganized speech or behavior, and/or unpleasant symptoms.

To get a full picture of the patient's state, the doctor may employ a physical examination, psychiatric assessment, blood laboratory testing, and imaging scans.

An important step in the diagnosis of schizophrenia is the screening and assessment of mental health. Schizophrenia symptoms can be confused with those of several other mental conditions, including bipolar disorder, schizoaffective disorder, anxiety disorders, severe depression, and substance misuse. To rule out these other illnesses, a doctor will do an examination.

CHAPTER 6

Drugs Used in the Treatment of Schizophrenia.

Many schizophrenia patients receive their initial therapy from antipsychotic drugs. To lessen or control the symptoms of schizophrenia, medications are frequently combined with other types of drugs. Several antipsychotic drugs are:

Aripiprazole (Abilify), olanzapine (Zyprexa), risperidone (Risperdal), quetiapine (Seroquel), ziprasidone (Geodon), and paliperidone (Invega)

Drugs for the treatment of
schizophrenia
Depression and mood swings are
frequent among people with
schizophrenia. There are various
sorts of drugs used besides
antipsychotics.

Among the mood stabilizers are:

Lamotrigine (Lamictal), lithium
(Lithobid), Divalproex (Depakote),
and carbamazepine (Tegretol) are
antidepressants.

Sertraline and fluoxetine (Zoloft)
paroxetine (Paxil) (Paxil)
escitalopram with citalopram
(Celexa) (Lexapro)
venlafaxine (Effexor) (Effexor)

desvenlafaxine (Pristiq) (Pristiq)
Bupropion with duloxetine
(Cymbalta) (Wellbutrin)

Psychosis Treatment Behavioral
and Social Interventions
Family psychoeducation:
Psychosocial therapies are crucial in
the treatment of schizophrenia.
Support from family members helps
patients recover and reduces the
likelihood of psychotic episodes
relapsing. When everyone in the
family knows how to support a loved
one who is suffering from
schizophrenia, family interactions
strengthen.

Psychosocial Interventions in the Treatment of Schizophrenia. Outpatient support groups are utilized in assertive community treatment (ACT), another type of psychosocial intervention. To help prevent the need for hospitalization or a decline in the mental status of the schizophrenia patient, support teams made up of psychiatrists, nurses, case managers, and other counselors visit often with them.

Psychosis Treatment Behavioral and Social Interventions Treatment for substance addiction: Up to 50% of patients with schizophrenia also struggle with substance usage. For improved results, these substance misuse problems must be treated because they exacerbate the behavioral signs of schizophrenia.

Psychosocial Interventions for Schizophrenia Treatment
Social skill development It's possible that people with schizophrenia need to relearn how to behave in social settings. This type of psychosocial intervention is practicing or acting out real-life scenarios so the person is ready for them when they arise. This kind of instruction can lessen drug usage and enhance interpersonal interactions.

Psychosocial Interventions for Schizophrenia Treatment
Supported employment: Due to their illness, many people with schizophrenia find it challenging to enter or reenter the workforce. This kind of psychosocial intervention supports persons with schizophrenia in creating their resumes, participating in job interviews, and even finding employers who will hire people with mental illnesses.

Psychosocial Interventions for Schizophrenia Treatment
Behavioral cognitive treatment (CBT): By changing their disruptive or harmful thought patterns, patients with schizophrenia may be able to

work more effectively. To recognize hallucinations or "voices" and to ignore them, patients might use this technique to "test" the veracity of their thoughts. Actively psychotic people may not benefit from this form of therapy, but it may be helpful for those who still experience symptoms that are bothersome after taking medication.

Psychosis Treatment Behavioral and Social Interventions
Weight control: A common side effect of several antipsychotic and psychiatric medications is weight gain. Exercise frequently, consume a healthy diet, and maintain a

healthy weight to help prevent or treat other medical conditions.

CHAPTER 7

What Is the Prognosis for Schizophrenia.

Depending on how much care and support a patient receives, their prognosis for schizophrenia can change. Many individuals who suffer from schizophrenia can function effectively and lead regular lives. On the other hand, substance usage and mortality rates are higher in those with schizophrenia. Patients may see better results when their meds are taken consistently and their families are encouraged.

(B)Disordered schizophrenia

Disorganized actions and sometimes odd or difficult-to-understand speech are signs of schizophrenia in the disorganized form. They might exhibit improper feelings or responses that have nothing to do with the current circumstance. Their chaotic mental patterns may cause disruptions to or disregard daily routines including eating, cleaning up, and working.

(C) Schizophrenia catatonic

Movement disturbances identify catatonic-type schizophrenia.

People who have this kind of schizophrenia might range from being completely motionless to moving all over the place. They might remain silent for hours or they might keep repeating whatever you say or do. Due to their frequent inability to care for themselves or carry out everyday tasks, these actions put these persons who have schizophrenia of the catatonic kind in high danger.

(D) Unilateral Schizophrenia

When a person displays behaviors that fall under two or more of the other categories of schizophrenia, such as delusions, hallucinations, disorganized speech or conduct, or catatonic behavior, this condition is referred to as undifferentiated-type schizophrenia.

Remaining schizophrenia

A person is said to have residual-type schizophrenia if they have experienced at least one episode of schizophrenia in the past but don't currently exhibit any symptoms (delusions, hallucinations, disordered speech, or behavior). The patient can be completely symptom-free or they might get them again at some point.

9 798372 609082